Betty
Sanchez
City
Library
EXP.10-2015

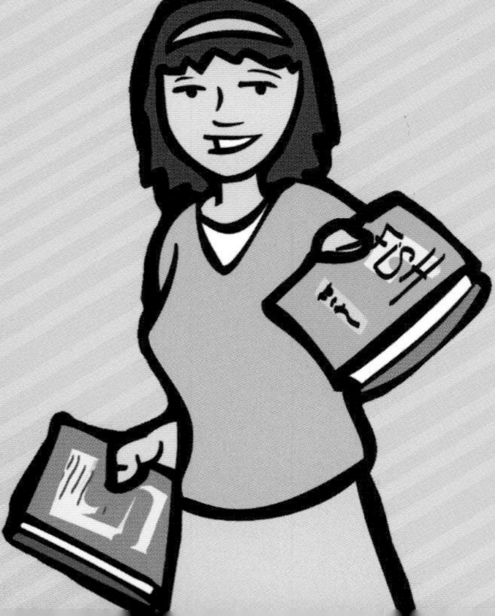
FISH

FIRST GRAPHICS

MY COMMUNITY

A VISIT TO THE LIBRARY

BY SARAH C. WOHLRABE

ILLUSTRATED BY
JEFFREY THOMPSON

Consultant: Diane R. Chen, Library Information Specialist
John F. Kennedy Middle School, Nashville, Tennessee

CAPSTONE PRESS
a capstone imprint

First Graphics are published by Capstone Press,
151 Good Counsel Drive, P.O. Box 669, Mankato, Minnesota 56002.
www.capstonepub.com

Books published by Capstone Press are manufactured with paper containing at least 10 percent post-consumer waste.

Library of Congress Cataloging-in-Publication Data
Wohlrabe, Sarah C., 1976-
A visit to the library / by Sarah C. Wohlrabe ; illustrated by Jeffrey Thompson.
p. cm. — (First graphics. My community)
Includes bibliographical references.
ISBN 978-1-4296-5371-8 (library binding)
ISBN 978-1-4296-6234-5 (paperback)
1. Libraries—Juvenile literature. 2. Libraries—Comic books, strips, etc. 3. Graphic novels. I. Thompson, Jeffrey (Jeffrey Allen), 1970- ill. II. Title. III. Series.

Z665.5.W64 2011
027—dc22

2010026744

Editor: **Shelly Lyons**
Designer: **Alison Thiele**
Art Director: **Nathan Gassman**
Production Specialist: **Eric Manske**

Printed in the United States of America in
Stevens Point, Wisconsin.
092010 005934WZS11

Betty Sanchez
City Library
EXP.10-2015

TABLE OF CONTENTS

Come Explore

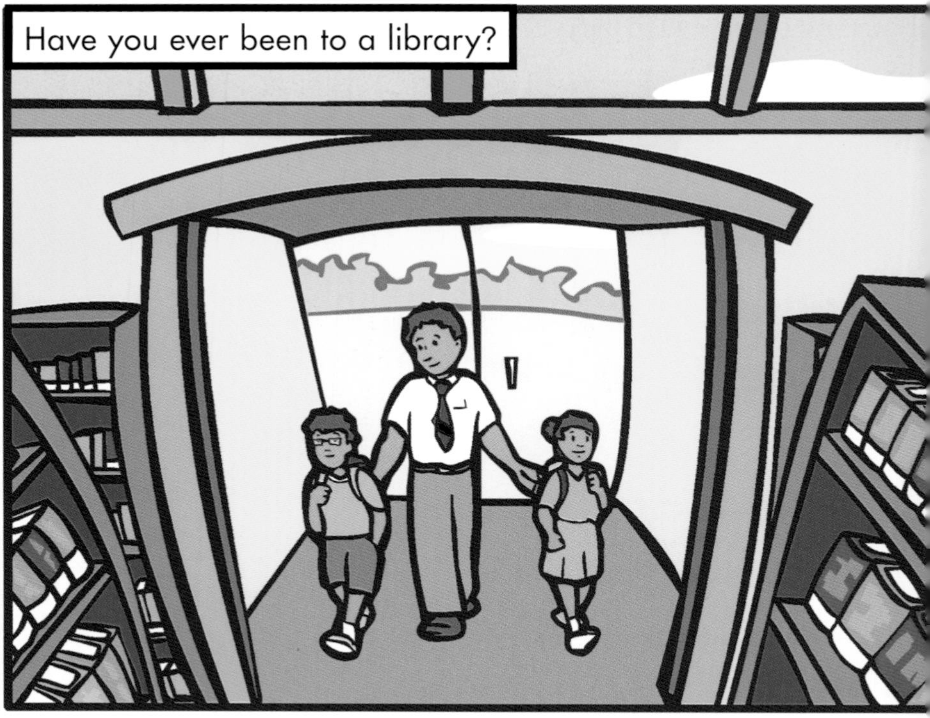
Have you ever been to a library?

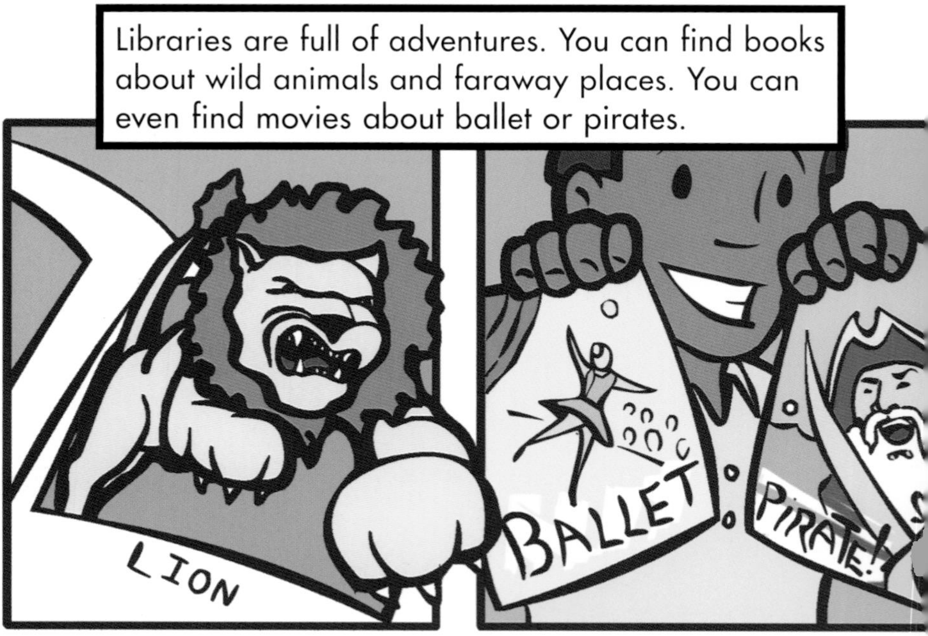
Libraries are full of adventures. You can find books about wild animals and faraway places. You can even find movies about ballet or pirates.
LION
BALLET
PIRATE!

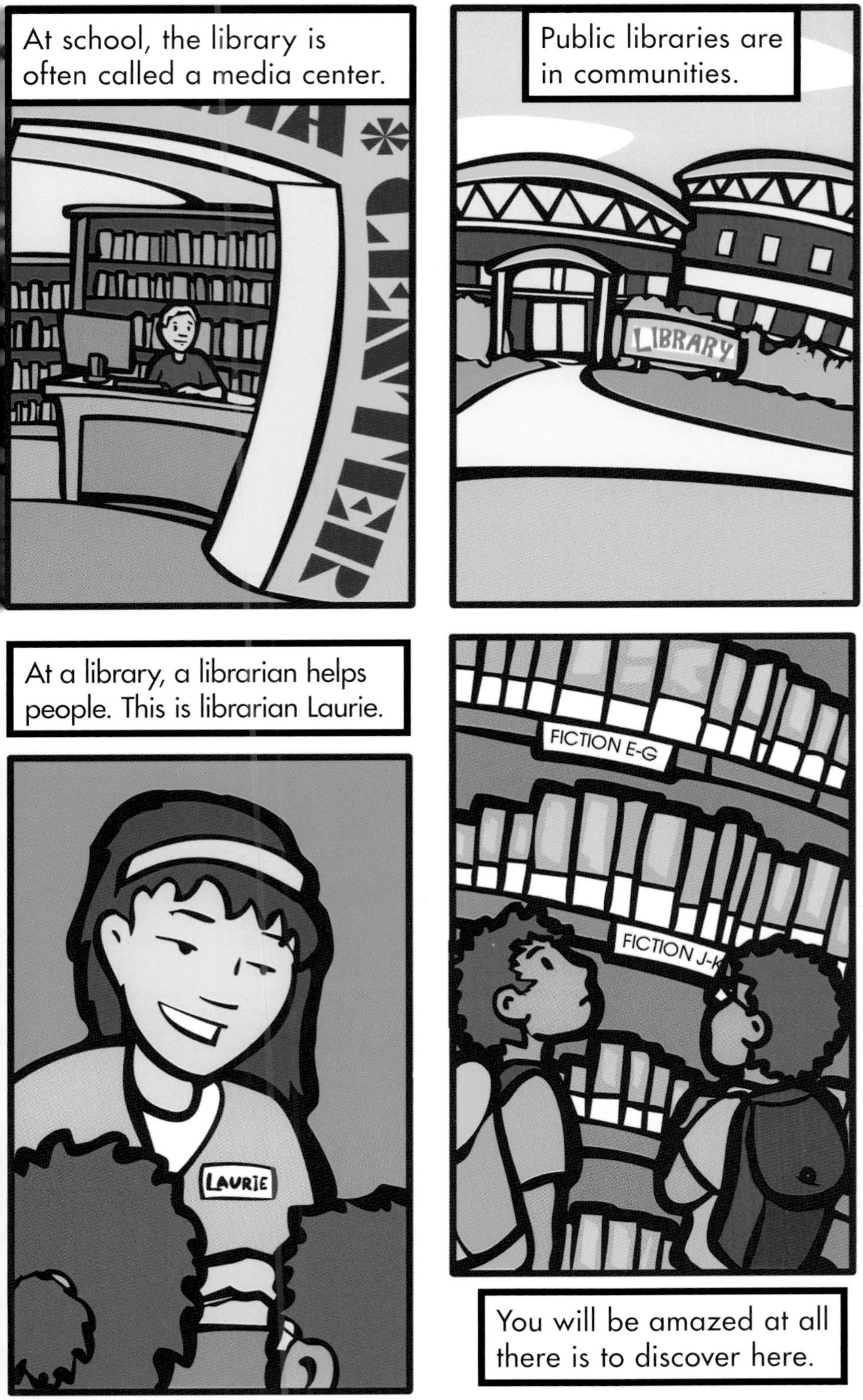
At school, the library is often called a media center.
MEDIA CENTER
Public libraries are in communities.
LIBRARY
At a library, a librarian helps people. This is librarian Laurie.
LAURIE
FICTION E-G
FICTION J-K
You will be amazed at all there is to discover here.

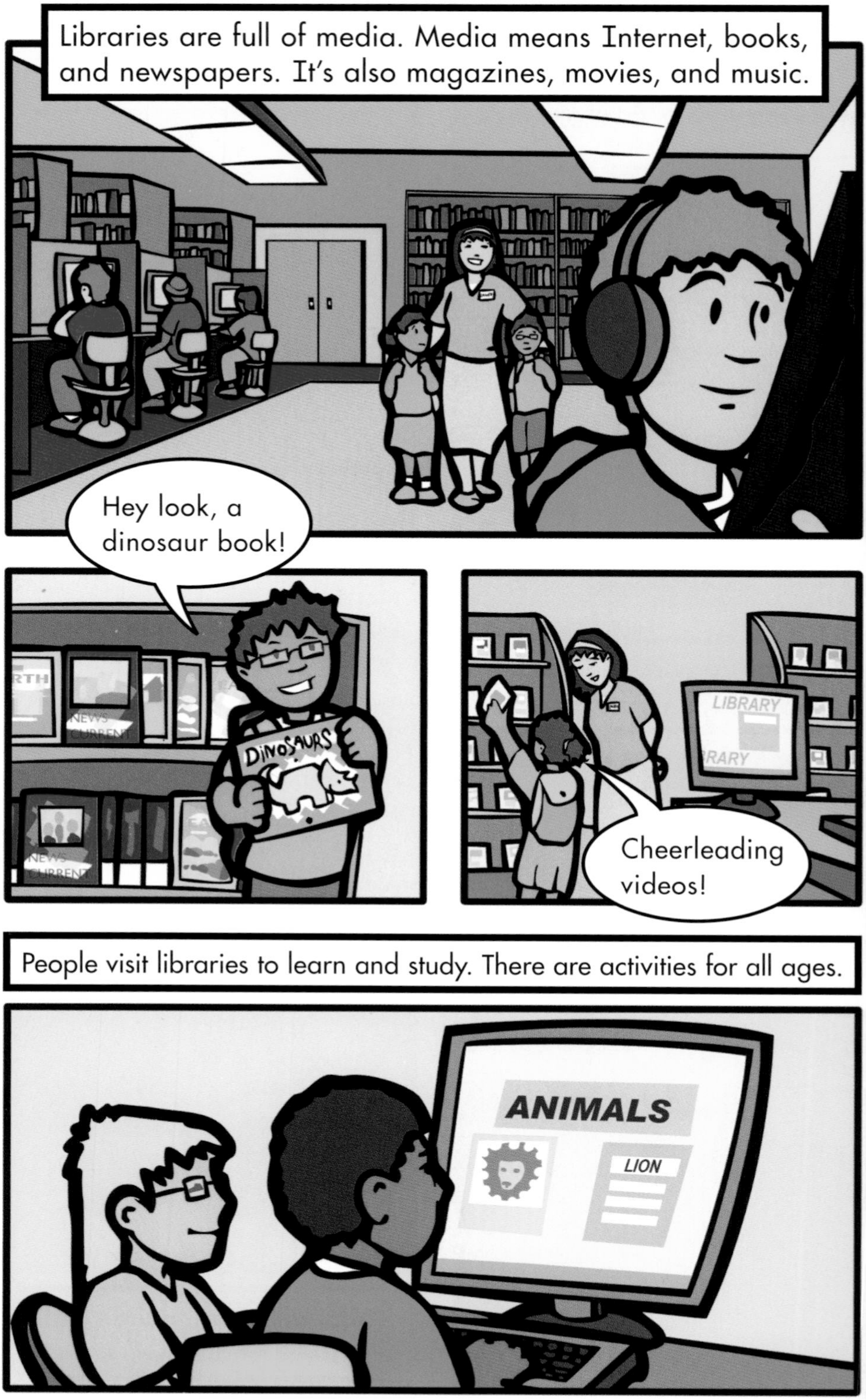
Libraries are full of media. Media means Internet, books, and newspapers. It's also magazines, movies, and music.
Hey look, a dinosaur book!
DINOSAURS
LIBRARY
Cheerleading videos!
People visit libraries to learn and study. There are activities for all ages.
ANIMALS
LION

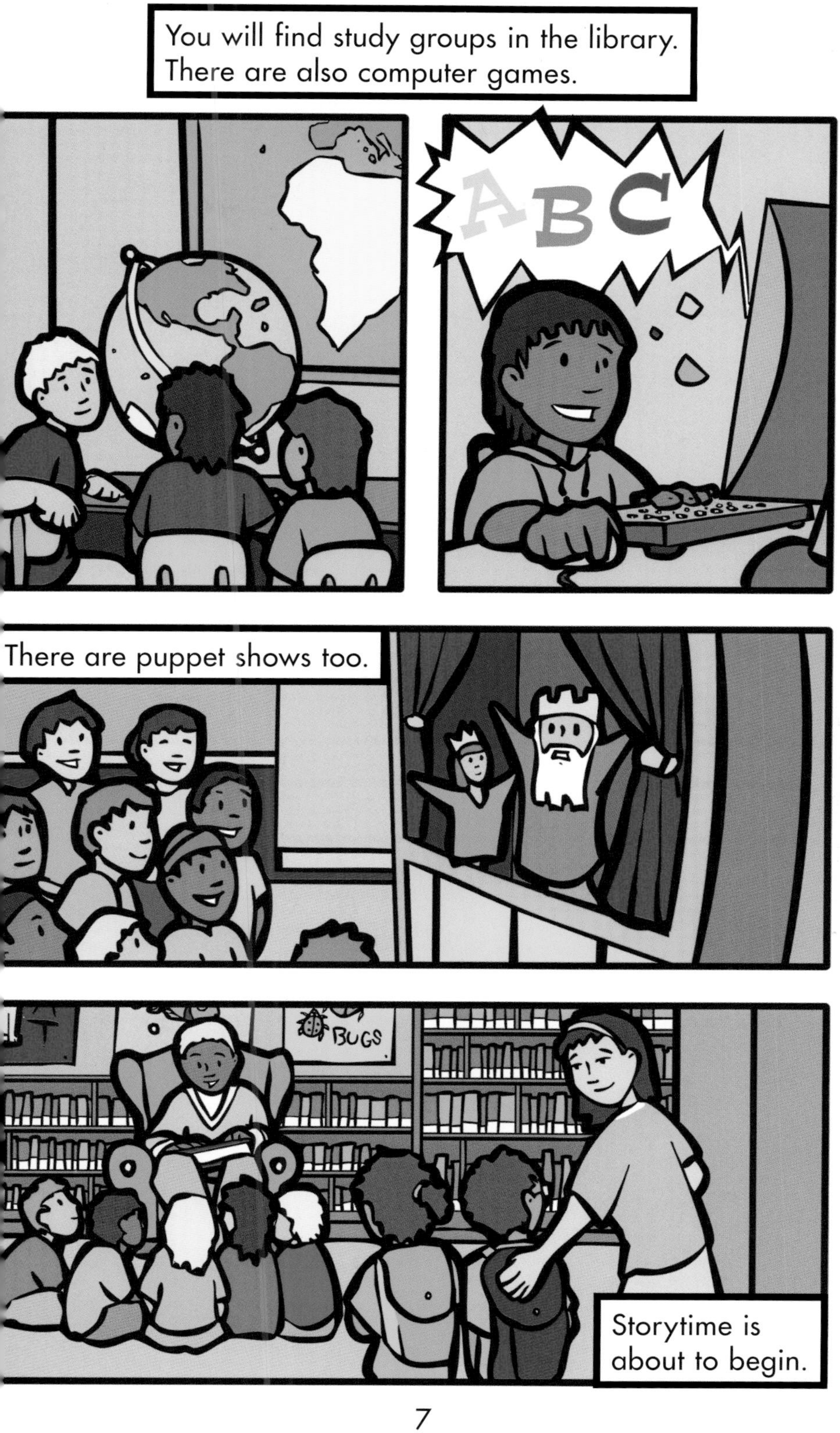
You will find study groups in the library.
There are also computer games.
ABC
There are puppet shows too.
BUGS
Storytime is
about to begin.

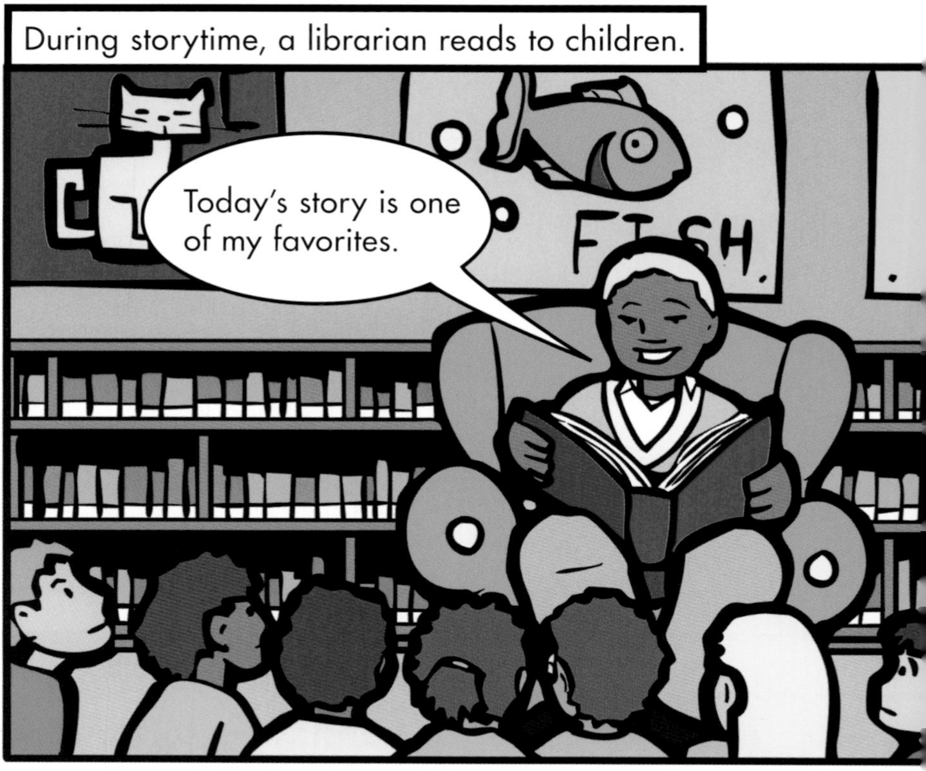
During storytime, a librarian reads to children.
Today's story is one of my favorites.

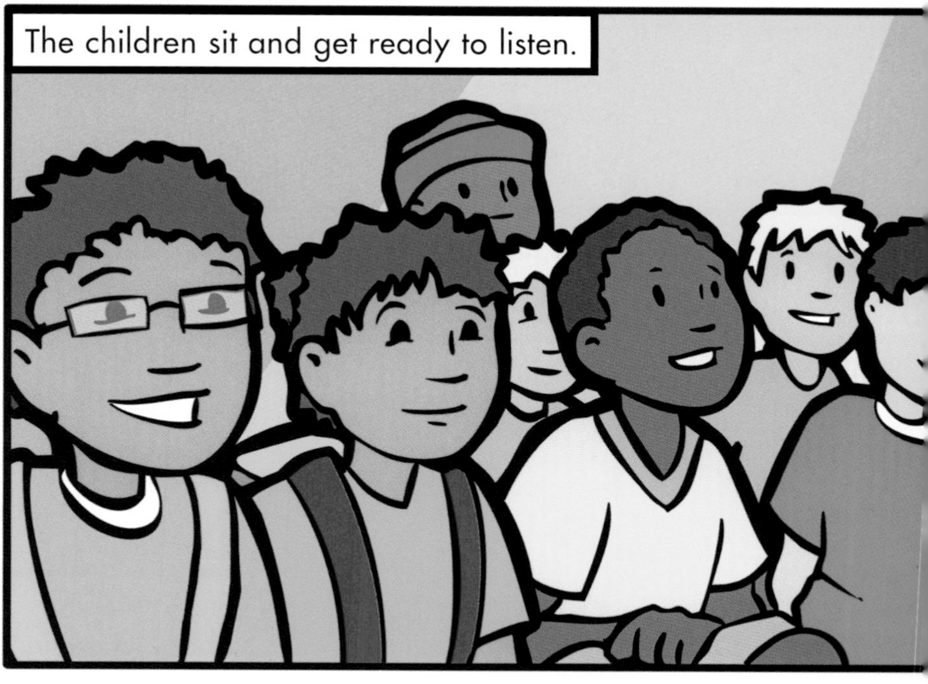
The children sit and get ready to listen.

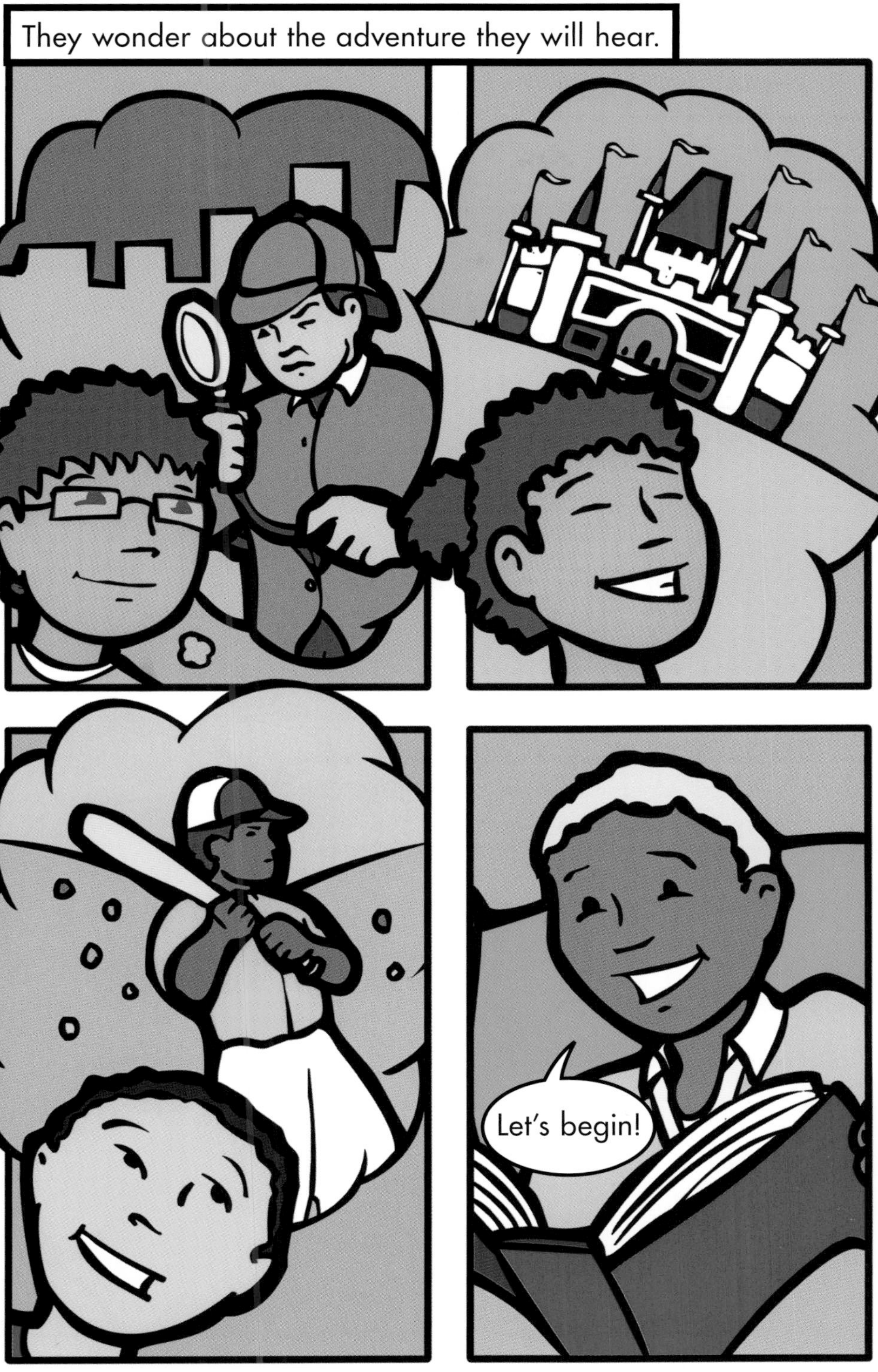
They wonder about the adventure they will hear.
Let's begin!

WHERE DO I FIND IT?

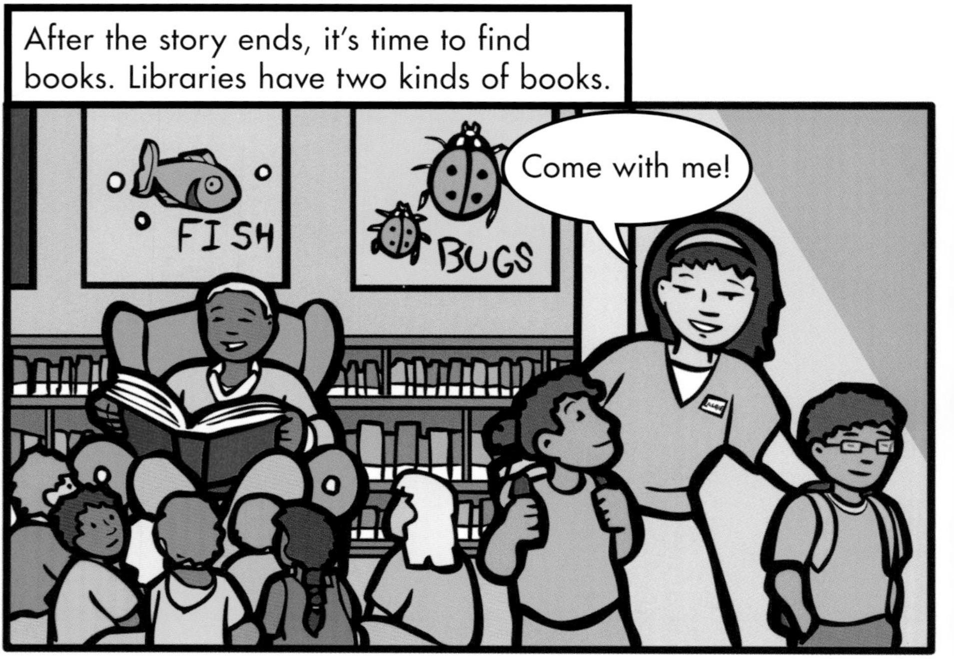
After the story ends, it's time to find books. Libraries have two kinds of books.
FISH
BUGS
Come with me!

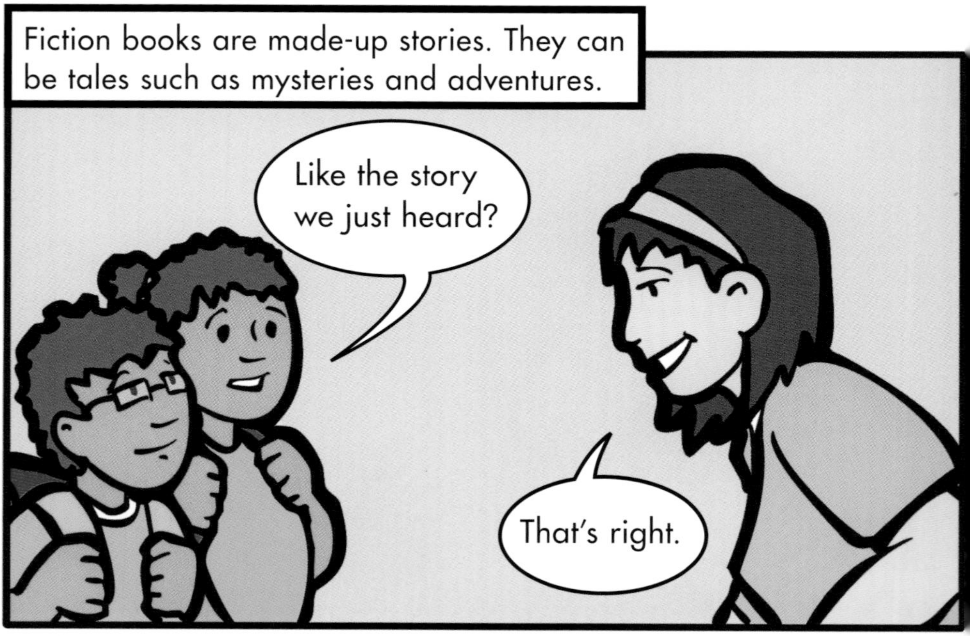
Fiction books are made-up stories. They can be tales such as mysteries and adventures.
Like the story we just heard?
That's right.

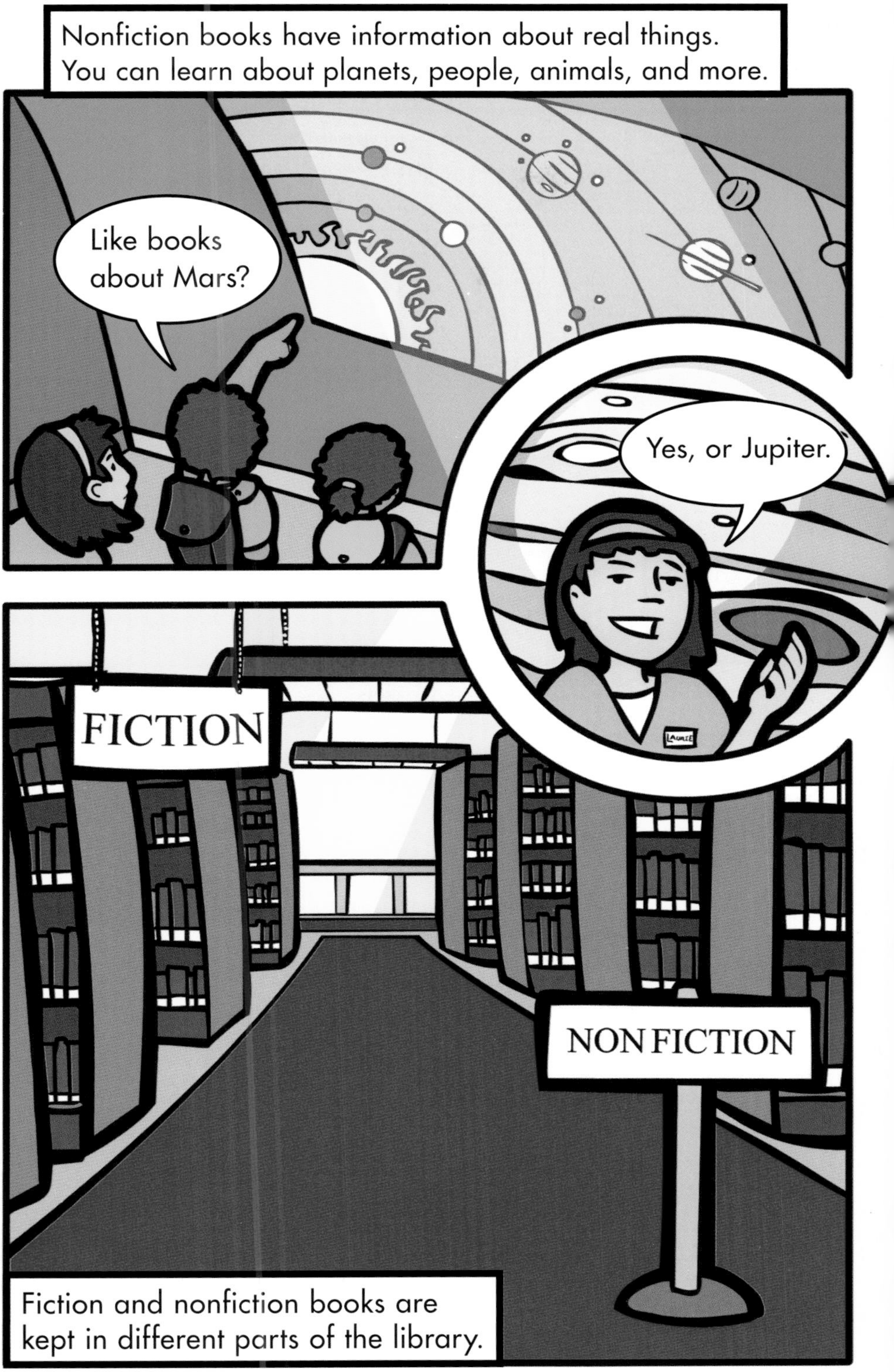
Nonfiction books have information about real things. You can learn about planets, people, animals, and more.
Like books about Mars?
Yes, or Jupiter.
FICTION
NONFICTION
Fiction and nonfiction books are kept in different parts of the library.

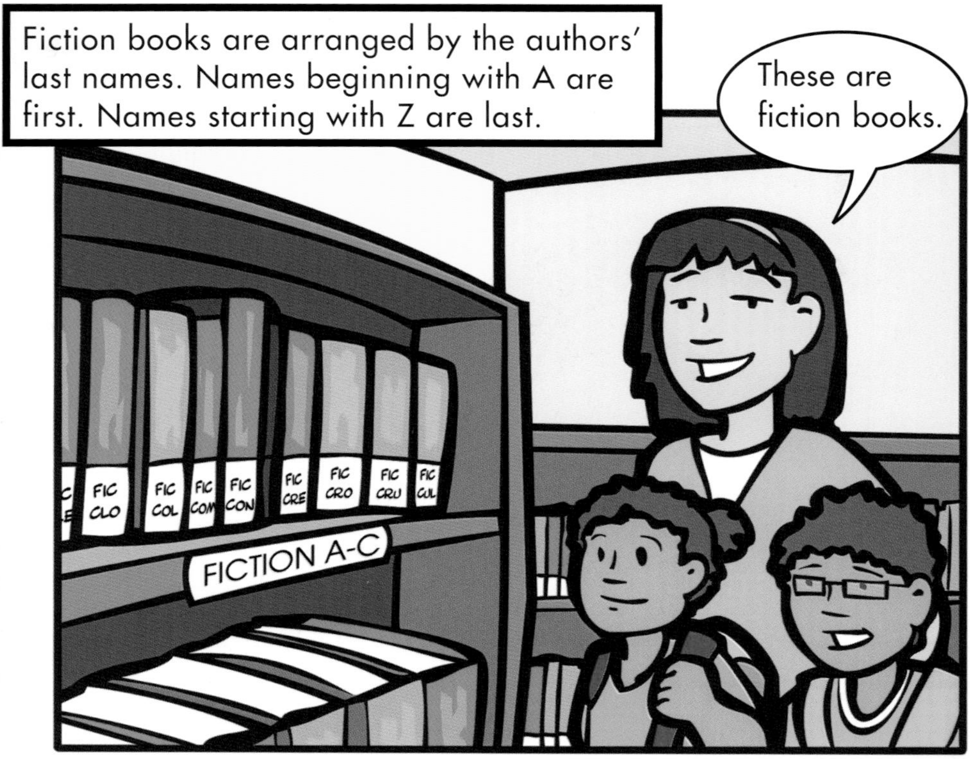
Fiction books are arranged by the authors' last names. Names beginning with A are first. Names starting with Z are last.
These are fiction books.
FICTION A-C

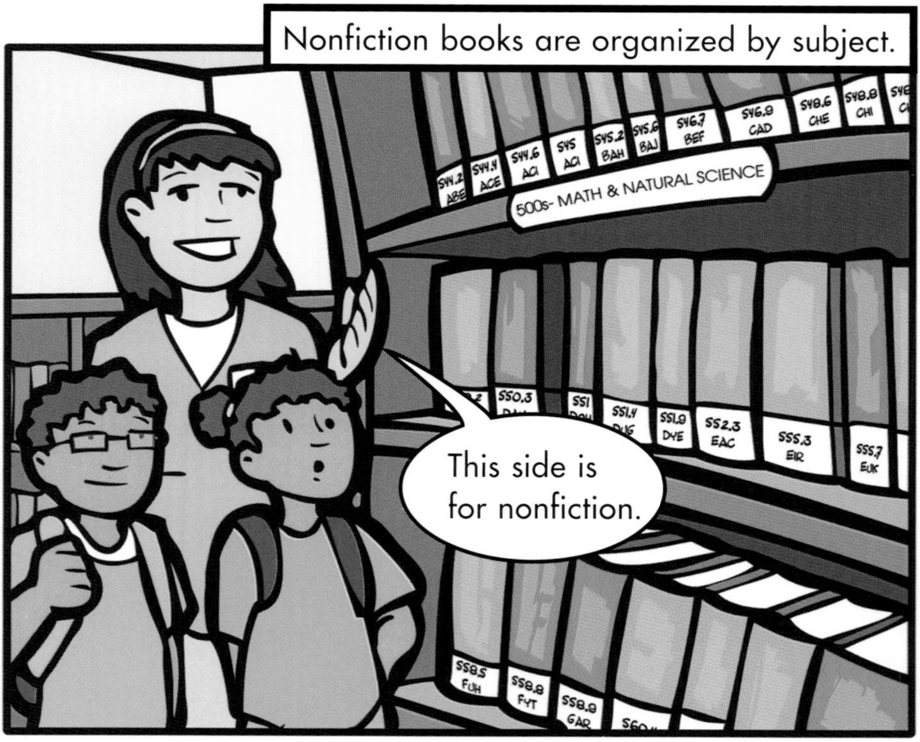
Nonfiction books are organized by subject.
500s- MATH & NATURAL SCIENCE
This side is for nonfiction.

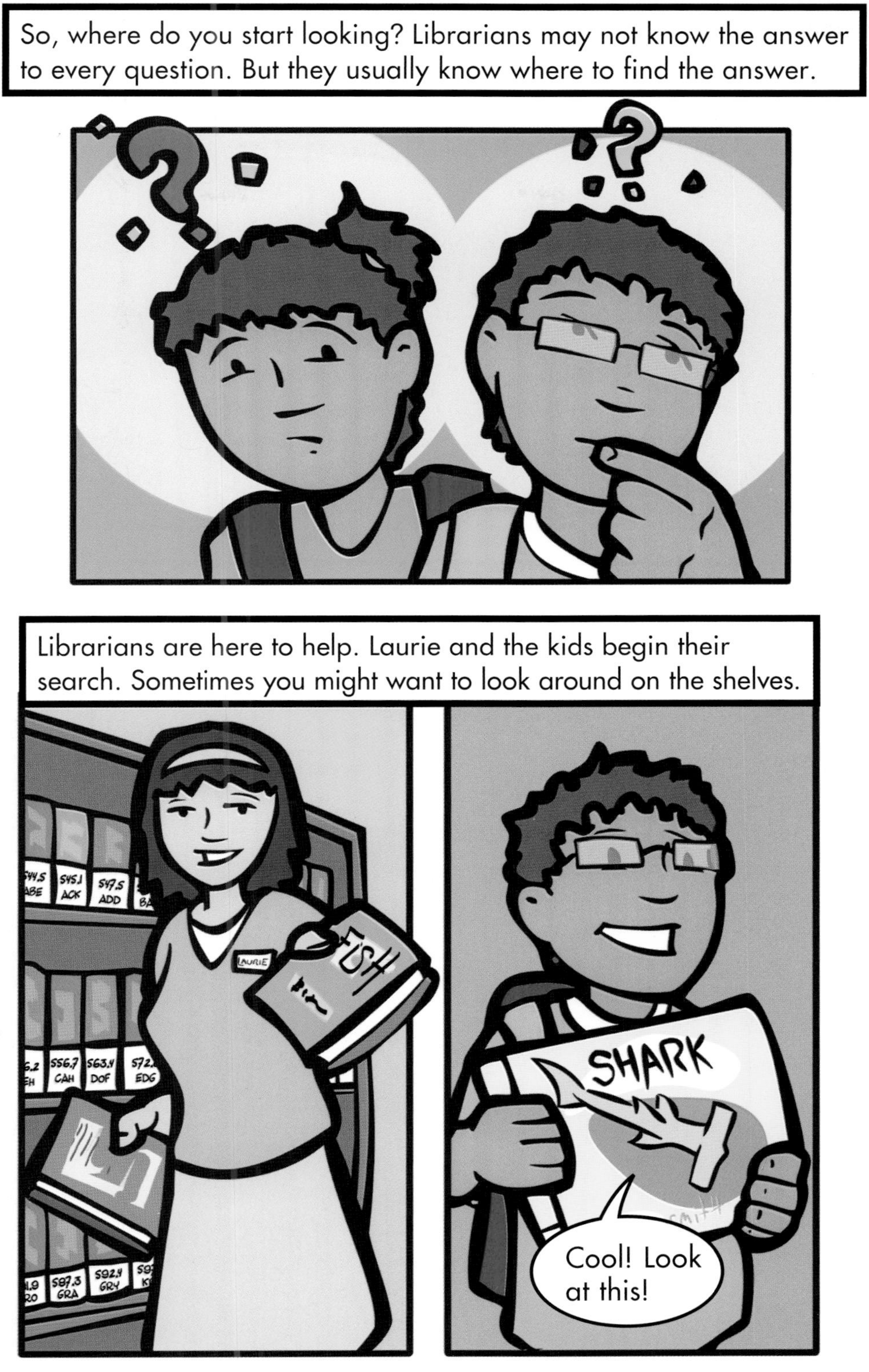
So, where do you start looking? Librarians may not know the answer to every question. But they usually know where to find the answer.
Librarians are here to help. Laurie and the kids begin their search. Sometimes you might want to look around on the shelves.
545.1 ACK
547.5 ADD
556.7 CAH
563.4 DOF
587.3 GRA
592.4 GRY
LAURIE
SHARK
Cool! Look at this!

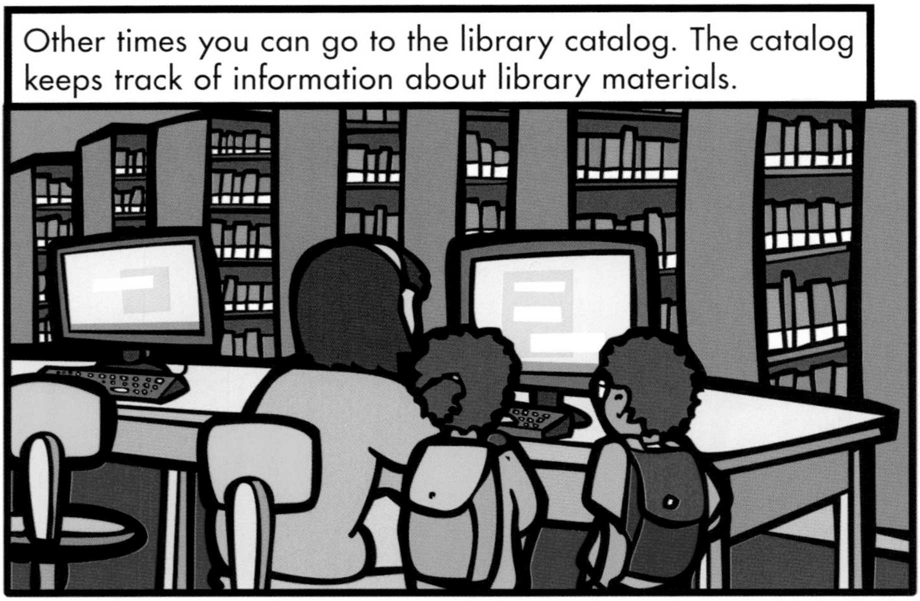
Other times you can go to the library catalog. The catalog keeps track of information about library materials.

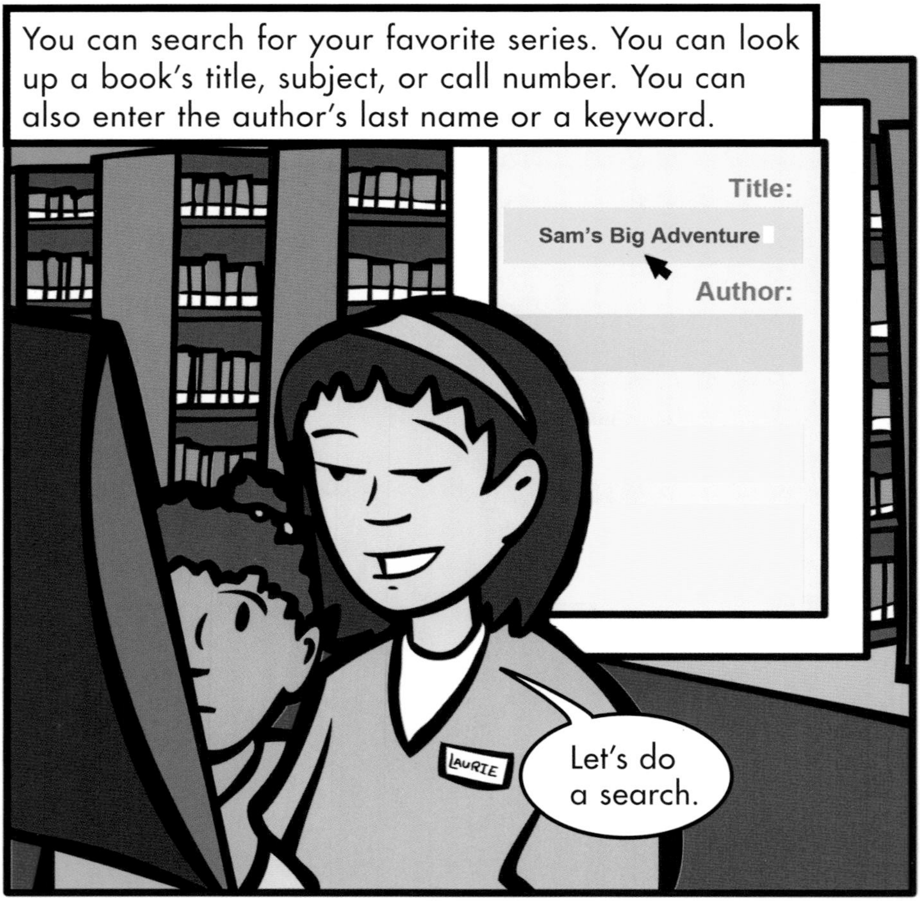
You can search for your favorite series. You can look up a book's title, subject, or call number. You can also enter the author's last name or a keyword.
Title:
Sam's Big Adventure
Author:
LAURIE
Let's do a search.

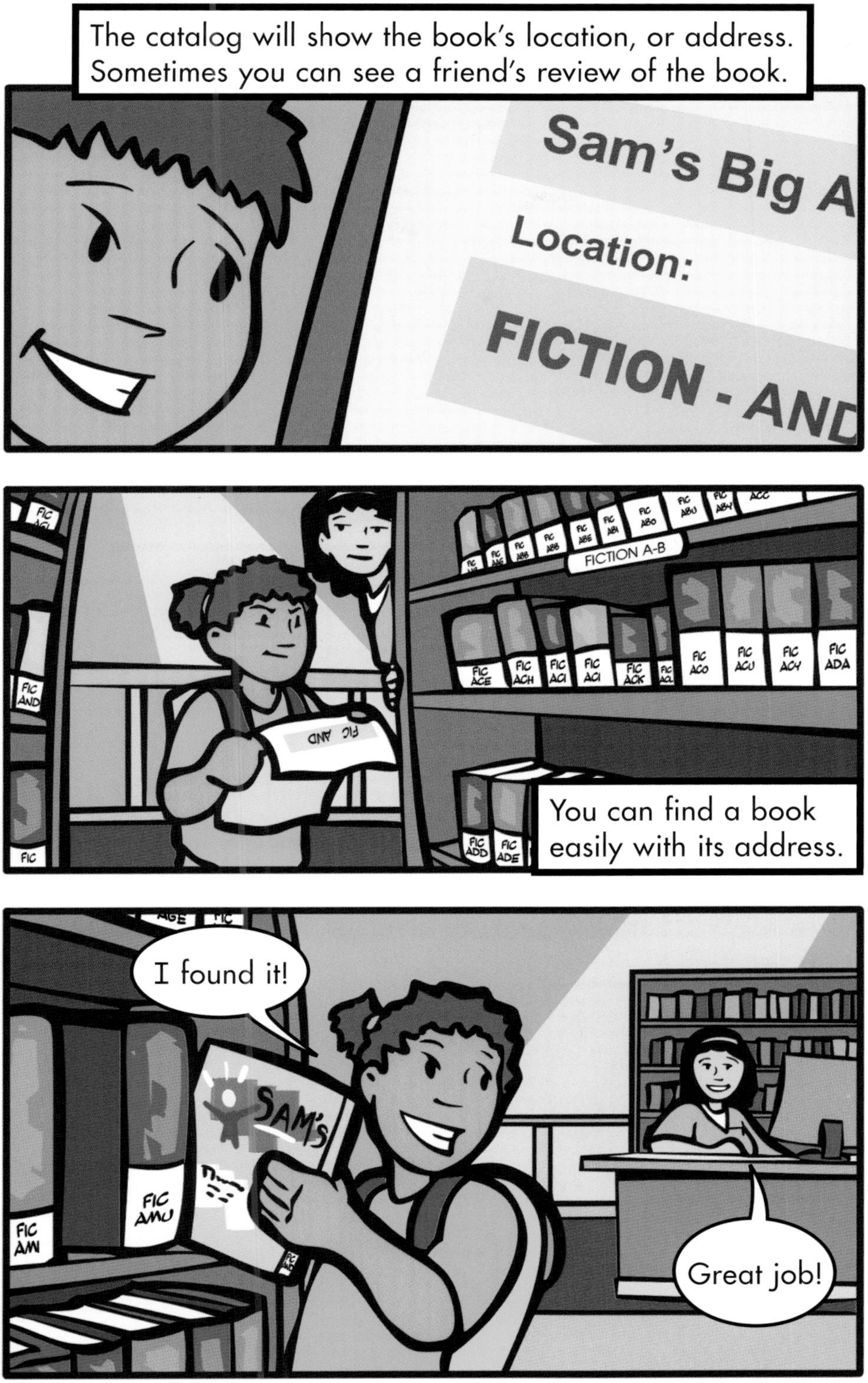
The catalog will show the book's location, or address. Sometimes you can see a friend's review of the book.
Sam's Big A
Location:
FICTION - AND
FICTION A-B
FIC AND
You can find a book easily with its address.
I found it!
SAM'S
Great job!

Laurie and the kids head to the nonfiction area. Nonfiction books are organized by the Dewey decimal system.

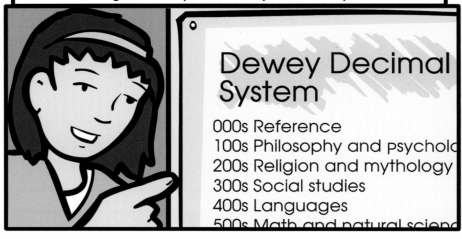

Dewey Decimal System

000s Reference
100s Philosophy and psycholo
200s Religion and mythology
300s Social studies
400s Languages
500s Math and natural scien

This system groups books together by subjects. Each book has a number and letters on its sticker.

Want a book on planets? The computer will give you a number in the 500s.

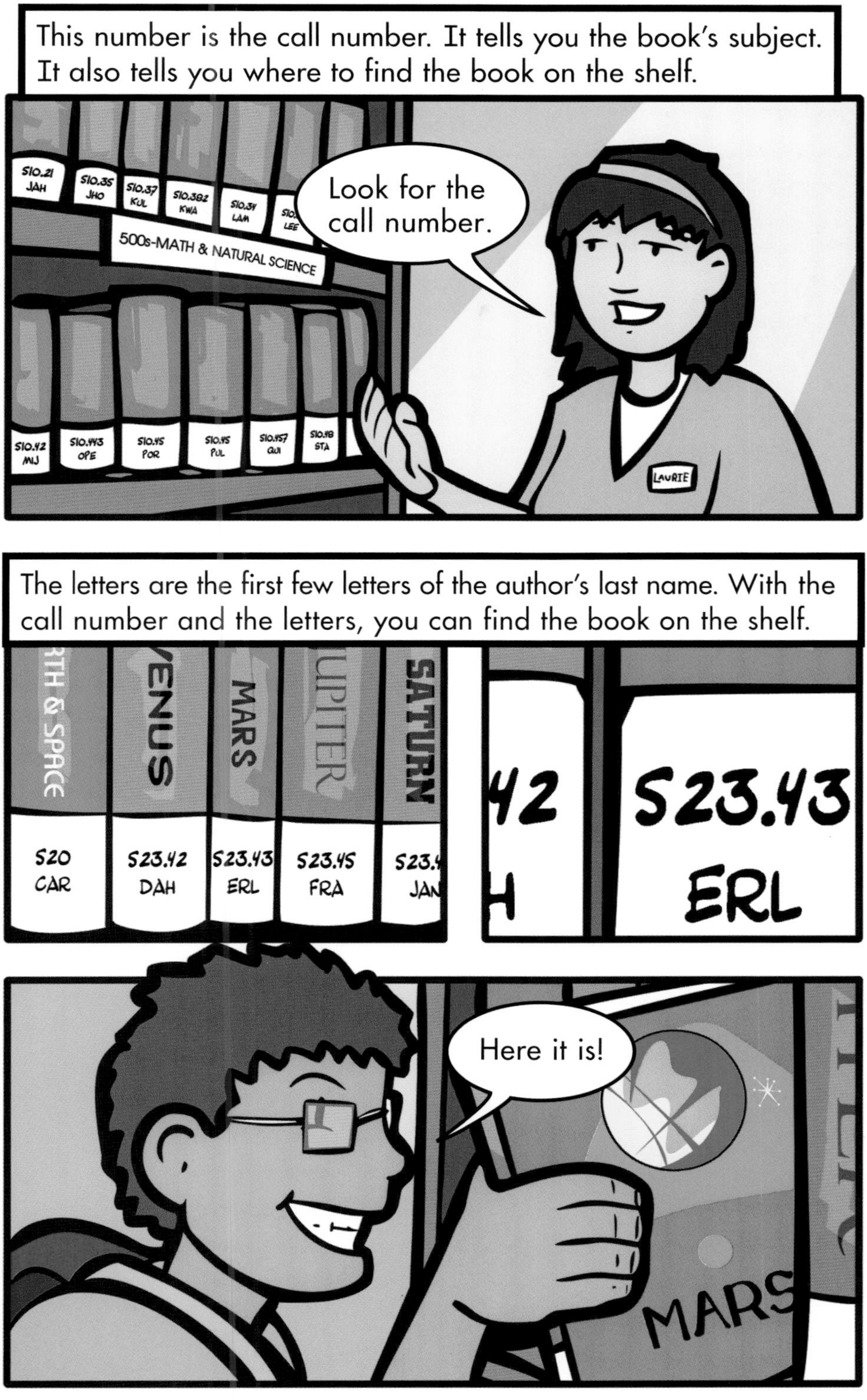
This number is the call number. It tells you the book's subject. It also tells you where to find the book on the shelf.
500s-MATH & NATURAL SCIENCE
Look for the call number.
LAURIE
The letters are the first few letters of the author's last name. With the call number and the letters, you can find the book on the shelf.
MARS
SATURN
520 CAR
523.42 DAH
523.43 ERL
523.45 FRA
523.43
ERL
Here it is!
MARS

CHECK IT OUT!

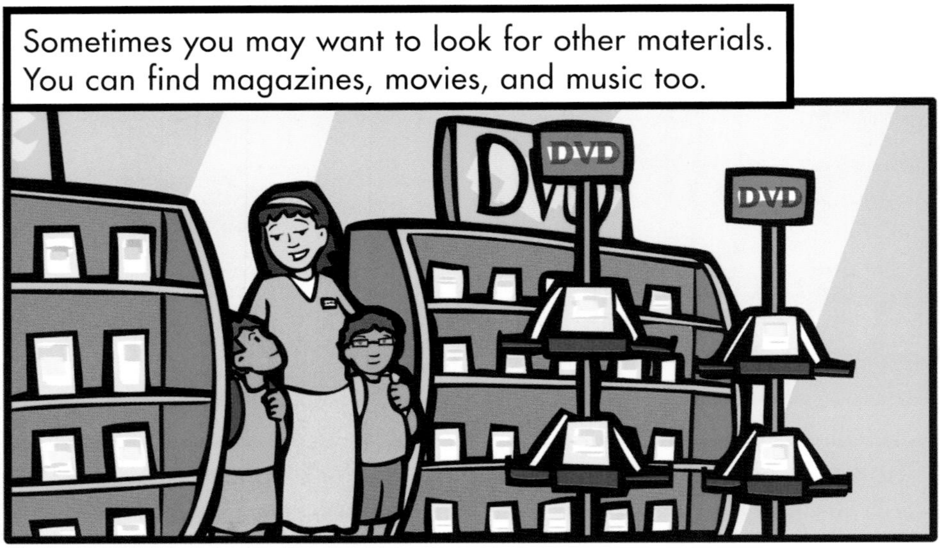
Sometimes you may want to look for other materials. You can find magazines, movies, and music too.
DVD
DVD

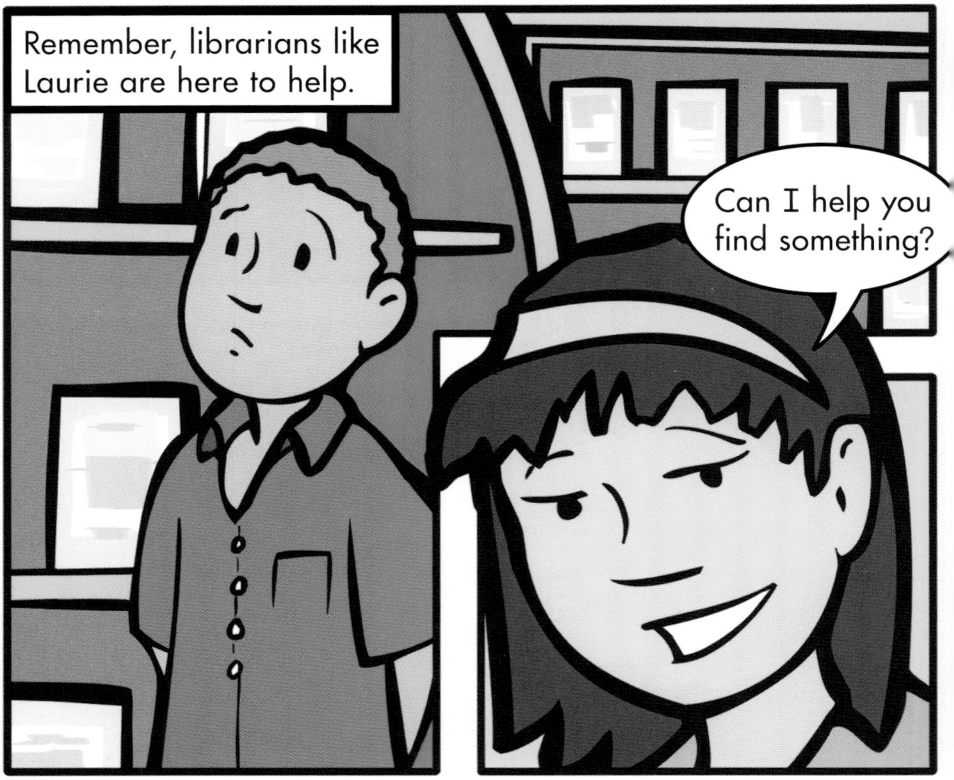
Remember, librarians like Laurie are here to help.
Can I help you find something?

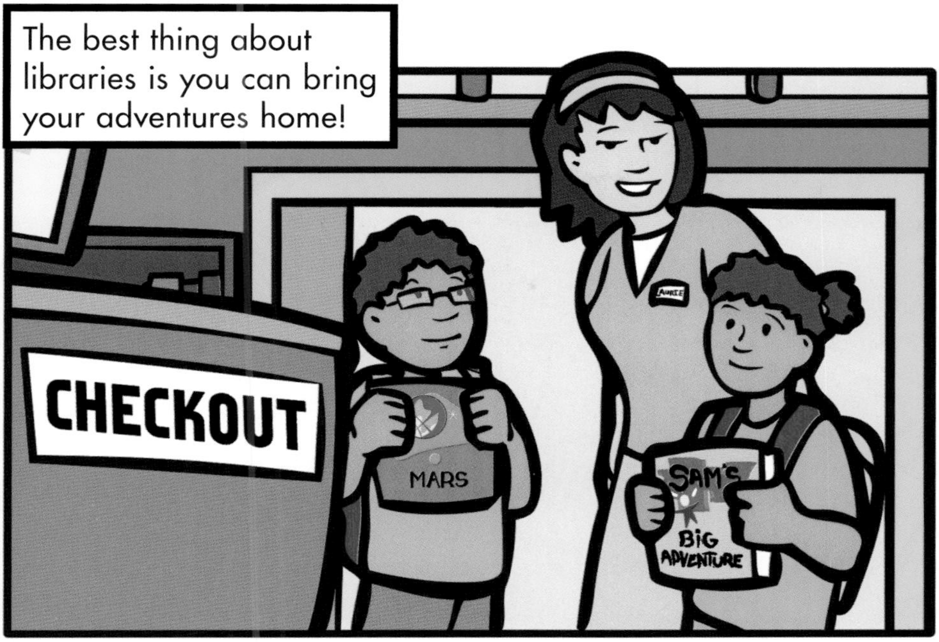
The best thing about libraries is you can bring your adventures home!
CHECKOUT
MARS
SAM'S BIG ADVENTURE

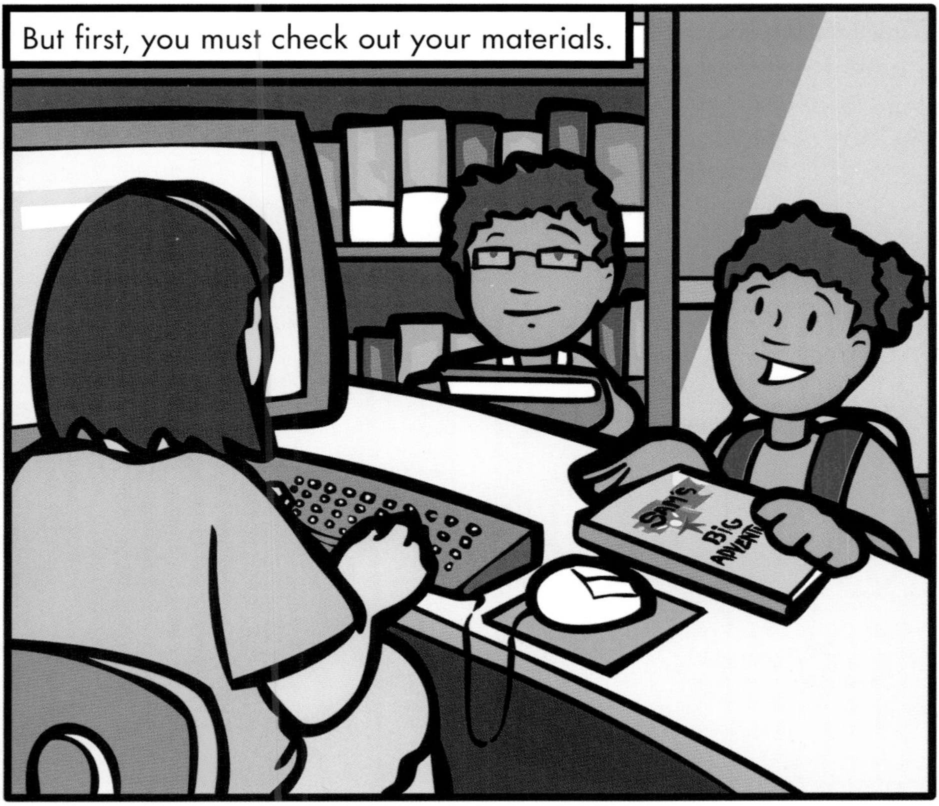
But first, you must check out your materials.

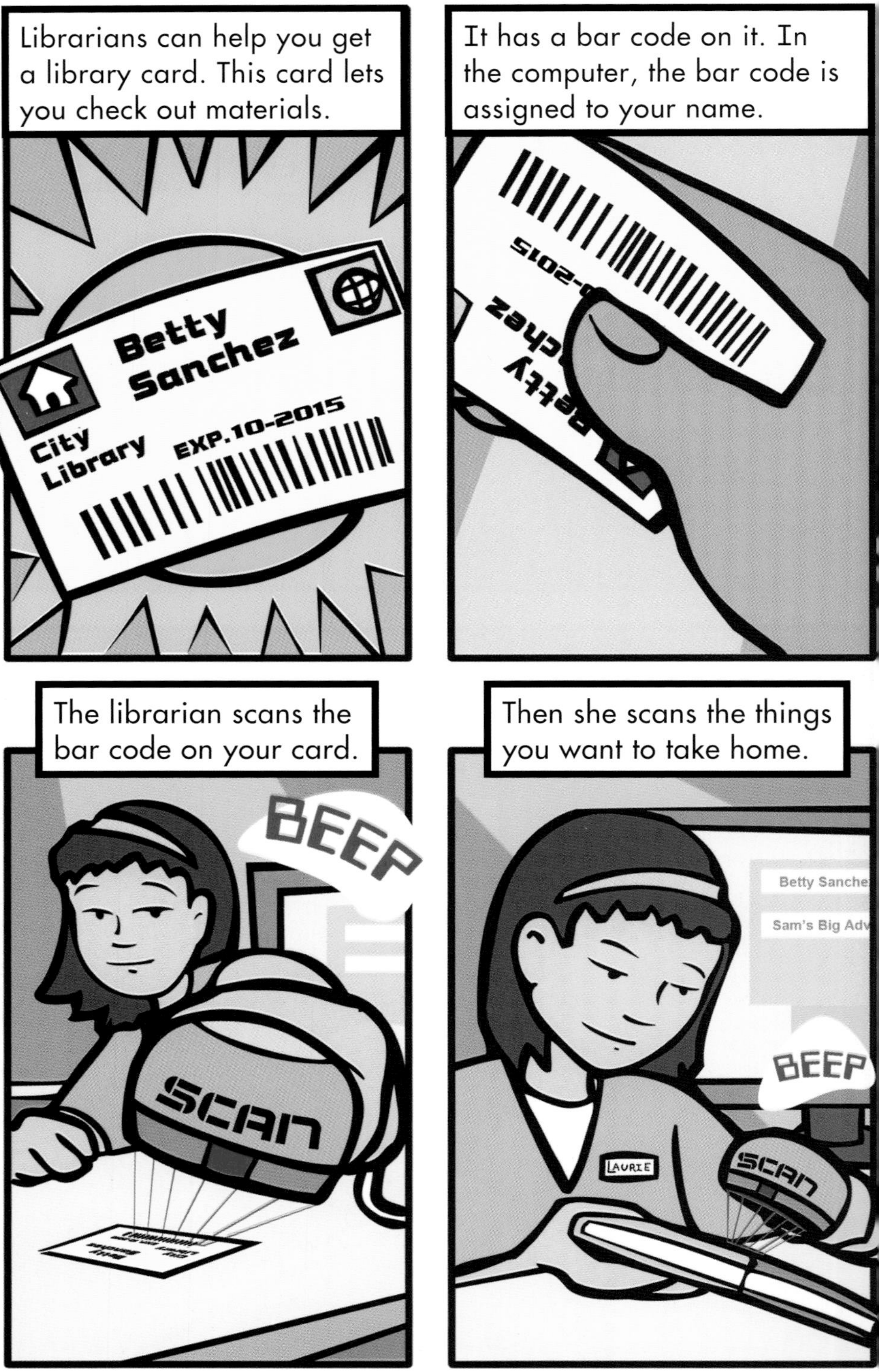
Librarians can help you get a library card. This card lets you check out materials.
Betty Sanchez
City Library
EXP.10-2015
It has a bar code on it. In the computer, the bar code is assigned to your name.
The librarian scans the bar code on your card.
BEEP
SCAN
Then she scans the things you want to take home.
BEEP
LAURIE
SCAN

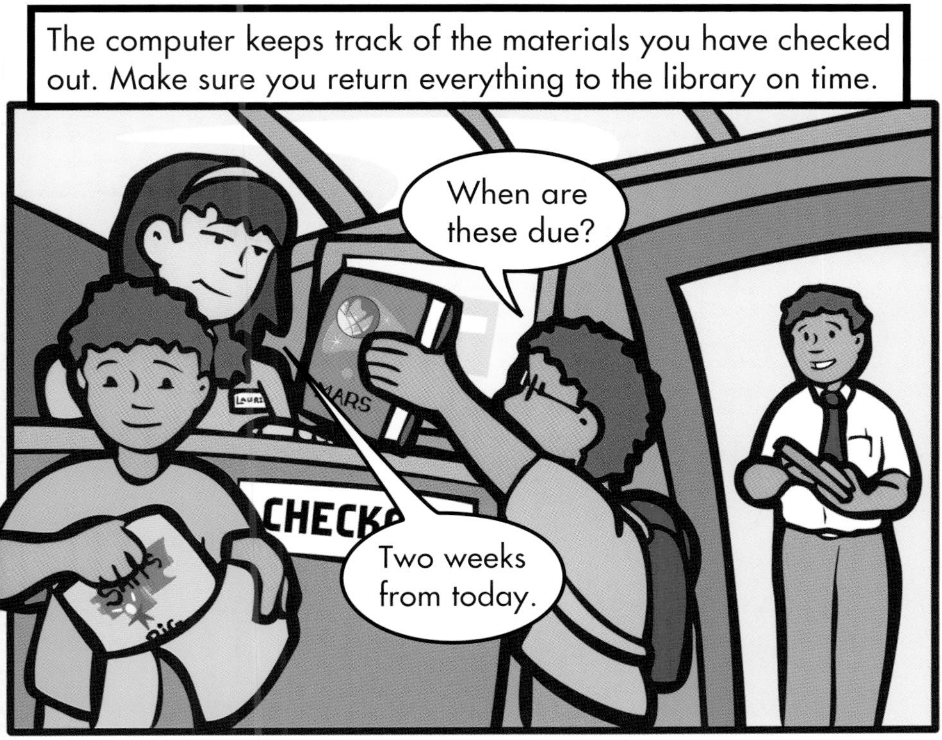
The computer keeps track of the materials you have checked out. Make sure you return everything to the library on time.
When are these due?
Two weeks from today.

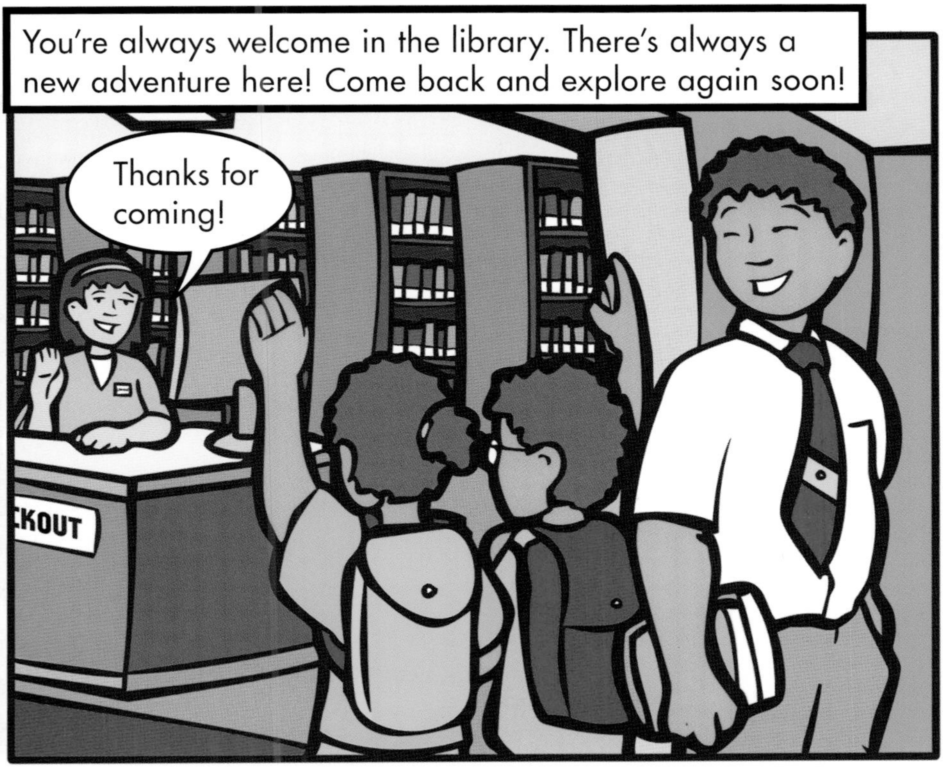
You're always welcome in the library. There's always a new adventure here! Come back and explore again soon!
Thanks for coming!

GLOSSARY

author—the person who wrote the book or article

bar code—a block of bars found on a book's back cover; librarians and booksellers scan the code to find out information about the book

call number—the series of numbers and letters that tells where a book is located in the library

Dewey decimal system—a way to organize books in a library

fiction—books that are made-up stories written by an author

library catalog—a computerized collection of all the materials in a library; materials can be found in the catalog by searching for titles, authors, subjects, keywords, or call numbers

media—items to gain information or a story from; newspapers, books, music, movies, and Internet are all media

nonfiction—books that are written by an author with the purpose of teaching something

READ MORE

Buzzeo, Toni. *The Library Doors.* Fort Atkinson, Wis.: Upstart Books, 2008.

Donovan, Sandy. *Bob the Alien Discovers the Dewey Decimal System.* In the Library. Minneapolis: Picture Window Books, 2010.

Finn, Carrie. *Manners in the Library.* Way to Be! Minneapolis: Picture Window Books, 2007.

INTERNET SITES

FactHound offers a safe, fun way to find Internet sites related to this book. All of the sites on FactHound have been researched by our staff.

Here's all you do:

Visit *www.facthound.com*

Type in this code: 9781429653718

Super-cool stuff!

Check out projects, games and lots more at
www.capstonekids.com

23

INDEX

MY COMMUNITY

TITLES IN THIS SET:

A DAY AT THE
FIRE STATION

GOING TO THE
DENTIST

TRANSPORTATION
IN THE CITY

A VISIT TO THE
LIBRARY

A VISIT TO THE
POLICE STATION

A VISIT TO THE
VET

WORKING ON THE
FARM

FIRST GRAPHICS

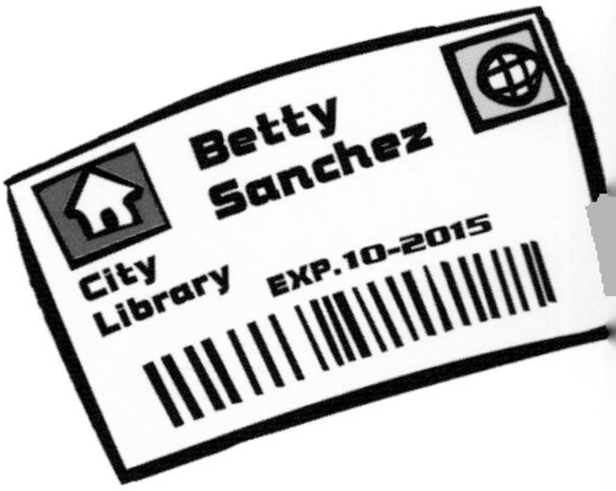
Betty Sanchez
City Library
EXP.10-2015